BX
4795

D1072439

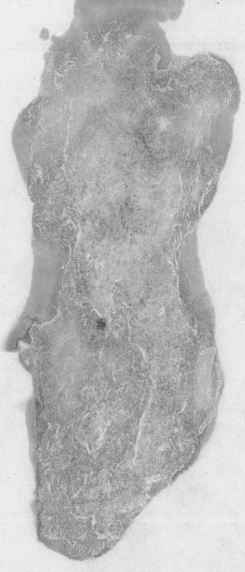

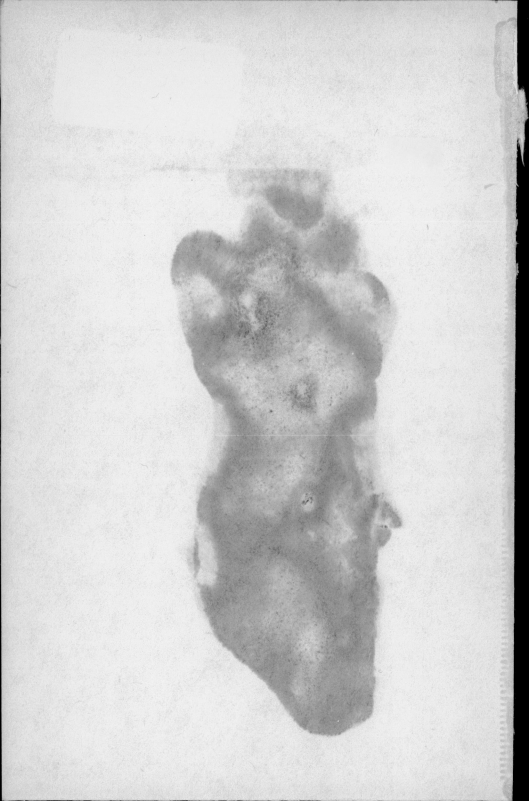

BYWAYS *of* HISTORY

". . . GOLD, AND SILVER, IVORY, AND APES, AND PEACOCKS."

I KINGS X: 22

THE LAND OF THE GREAT IMAGE
Being Experiences of Friar Manrique in ARAKAN
by *MAURICE COLLIS*

> I found that I could not put it down — I recommend it to all readers who, sharing my state of mind, might welcome a journey into a strange pocket of history.
>
> CLIFTON FADIMAN
> in the *New Yorker*

CARDINAL OF SPAIN
The Life and Strange Career of ALBERONI
by *SIMON HARCOURT–SMITH*

THE LAND OF PRESTER JOHN
A Chronicle of Portuguese Exploration
by *ELAINE SANCEAU*

THESE ARE BORZOI BOOKS, PUBLISHED BY
ALFRED A. KNOPF

B.09.
alberoni

c.1 Special Purchase 2/1/63

CARDINAL OF SPAIN

The Life and Strange Career of ALBERONI

CARDINAL OF SPAIN

THE LIFE AND STRANGE CAREER OF

Alberoni

Simon Harcourt-Smith

ALFRED A KNOPF : NEW YORK

1944

BX
4705
.A44
H3

POINT PARK JUNIOR COLLEGE LIBRARY

THIS BOOK HAS BEEN PRODUCED
IN FULL COMPLIANCE
WITH ALL GOVERNMENT REGULATIONS
FOR THE CONSERVATION OF PAPER, METAL,
AND OTHER ESSENTIAL MATERIALS

Copyright 1944 by Simon Harcourt-Smith. All rights reserved. No part of this book may be reproduced in any form without permission in writing from the publisher, except by a reviewer who may quote brief passages or reproduce not more than three illustrations in a review to be printed in a magazine or newspaper. Manufactured in the United States of America.

FIRST AMERICAN EDITION

44 - 4829

FOR CHARLES

Families when a child is born,

Want it to be intelligent.

I *through intelligence*

Having wrecked my whole life

Only hope the baby will prove

Ignorant and stupid.

Thus he will crown a tranquil life

By *becoming a Cabinet Minister.*

SU TUNG-P'O, A.D. 1056–1101

"The character of the Germans is to be insolent and unbearable when things are going well for them; they would do well to reflect that Fortune by her very nature is capricious, and that there's nothing fixed under the moon." ALBERONI

PREFACE

WHEN this book was first envisaged, some four years ago, I hoped by researches at Simancas, Vienna, and in the Vatican Library to increase the store of original material on Alberoni already assembled by eminent French and Italian scholars. The outbreak of war exploded this ambition, and the study now presented can claim the prestige of few fresh sources. Conceiving the impact of Alberoni upon his times and future ages to be of more importance for example than a detailed investigation of the charges brought against his private life after his fall in 1720, I have tried, above all, to set Alberoni's life properly on the stage of his period; and to show that it was no mere extravagant five minutes of knock-about, but a momentous episode in the development of that strangely unknown period which immediately followed the victories of Marlborough. It was indeed an event that changed the whole history of the Mediterranean. An eminent English historian of the last century once suggested that had England not spurned the offer of Alberoni's friendship, the American colonies might never have been lost. It is a human tendency of the biographer to inflate the importance of his hero almost until there is no room left for any other history. That is the worst service I could do Alberoni — and his lively shade would not thank me for it. But I do believe that if we had not thwarted his precocious Italian nationalism and ruined his enterprise against Sicily in 1719, the Mussolini family would still be bound to their anvil and bellows, and our tragic onslaught on Italy in 1943, to free it once more of the loathed Germans, would have been unnecessary.

Until we come to the age of Gladstone, there never was in modern times a group of public men so enigmatical as those with which this book is concerned. Chatham, heroic for all his careful showmanship, Turgot, almost too gifted and too well intentioned for this world, Metternich repressing his turbulent thoughts no less severely than he repressed his turbulent Italians — here are calculable figures. But Louis XIV? Can one dismiss so Homeric a force with that cocksure spleen which Thackeray acquired in a day's excursion to Versailles? What was the real nature of the Regent? Inept libertine? Thwarted hero? And Alberoni himself? The Satanic genius of Frederick the Great's imagination? The noble statesman whom Voltaire and Fleury applauded? The buffoon of Saint-Simon's portrait? Upon those well-known but still mysterious features I have endeavoured to play an unexpected light, here bringing out a cheekbone, there emphasizing a pendant lip which may be clues to the puzzle.

As a matter of detail, it may be objected that my bias is unduly against the British policy of the time. But this tragicomedy is played almost entirely on a Continental stage. I have tried therefore to give the Continental reaction provoked by Stanhope's somewhat equivocal manœuvres. Many Englishmen are hurt and incredulous when told that we are not always beloved abroad. Many of our most tragic mistakes, I believe, spring from the inability to understand that not all honest men breathing necessarily feel affection for us. But it is difficult to lead the world and be its sweetheart at the same time.

In conclusion, I wish to tender my respectful gratitude to H. M. Queen Mary for her gracious assistance; and my thanks to the Duchess of Beaufort, the Spanish Embassy, the British Museum, the Victoria & Albert Museum, the London Library, the *Burlington Magazine*, the Bibliothèque Nationale of Paris, the Archives of the Quai d'Orsay, the Bibliothèque Royale of

Brussels, and the Alberonian College at Piacenza for the facilities which they were good enough to accord me. To Mr. Mervyn Saville's scholarship and energy my debt is incalculable. The Marquise de la Moussaye provided me with precious data on the obscurer details of Vendôme's career. Above all, my wife's numerous and valuable suggestions when the book was being conceived, her patient assistance in its final stages, cannot be repaid in a few trite words.

S. H-S.

LINSMEAU 1939 — BEMBRIDGE 1943

CONTENTS

ILLUSTRATIONS

ILLUSTRATIONS

CARDINAL OF SPAIN

The Life and Strange Career of ALBERONI

THE STAGE IS SET FOR ALBERONI

IF AN ANGEL wheeling down out of space any morning in the last years of the seventeenth century had paused in his flight to survey western Europe, he would have been offered in England and in France a spectacle that save for details has little changed to this day: two great kingdoms with their feet already planted on the road toward what, if only for convenience' sake, we still call sanity and progress: a world in short which was already "modern."

London with its bustling streets and coffee-houses, the Exchange and the new Bank of England a welter of money-making, Parliament blindly reducing the armed forces. At Drury Lane the pit hissed off the *Way of the World* with all the savagery that only the great, the incomprehensible can excite. Reaching up river — that river that held London in its toils — came East Indiamen heavy with ginger and ambergris, chocolate, silk, and porcelain, bearing the whole world in their thunderous sails.

These things are not after all very far removed from today. In one respect only was the difference radical: the great dome of St. Paul's was still little more than a splendid bubble on Wren's drawing board; and as the angel flew away out of the sea-coal smoke and the bright new spires, he would have seen but the drum rising like some lofty gasometer out of its scaffolding at the top of Ludgate Hill.

Surveying the face of France, he would have lit upon a state of things even nearer perhaps to us in spirit and appearance. An industrious and thriving population, by not many millions inferior to the present one: Paris the temple of elegance, of gloves ingeniously scented, silk stockings (for both women and men) of magical fineness, the latest dance, the latest fashion "in the nice conduct of a clouded cane." For the other side of the picture, the bayonets which flowed in a hundred sparkling streams through the towns toward the Belgian and German frontiers, proclaimed a military power apparently invincible; and as a complement to it, an administrative machine which in its passion for centralization, and its dragooning of commerce, strangely presaged the totalitarian.

At the controls of this formidable engine sat a man who, despite his Medici and Habsburg blood, personified the nation he ruled: hard-working, extrovert, honouring for all his Christian piety but one god — Reason; esteeming France as the supreme monument to that divinity; as ill-informed as ever a modern Frenchman is of what other nations might be thinking, and regarding all enemies of France as criminal lunatics; troubled as yet by nothing save his gout, which sprang from causes as French as he.

Turning southward, the heavenly witness would, however, soon be looking down upon a very different scene, upon another and vanished age; indeed he might have been tempted to wonder whether such a world had ever really existed outside the fancy of a Princess de Cleves [1] or of a Perrault; for such a confusion of abject pride and noble baseness, of valour and sloth, of necromancy and devotion as Spain presented at the close of the seventeenth century was rare enough in European history.

Already at Bayonne, the last considerable town before the frontier, there was a hint of what was to come. The ardours of

[1] See for example *Le Grand Cyrus*, a typical romantic novel of the period, running to a prodigious length. Mrs. Pepys would recite long passages of it, to vex her husband.

4